Wedding Invitations

QUARRY

HOW DO I LOVE THEE?

LET ME COUNT THE WAYS

—*Elizabeth Barrett Browning*

THE ARTFUL
BRIDE

Wedding Invitations

A STYLISH BRIDE'S GUIDE TO SIMPLE, HANDMADE WEDDING CORRESPONDENCE

GLOUCESTER MASSACHUSETTS

QUARRY BOOKS

LAURA McFADDEN AND APRIL L. PAFFRATH

First published in the United States of America by
Quarry Books, an imprint of
Rockport Publishers, Inc.
33 Commercial Street
Gloucester, Massachusetts 01930-5089
Telephone: (978) 282-9590
Fax: (978) 283-2742
www.rockpub.com

Library of Congress Cataloging-in-Publication Data
Paffrath, April L.
    The artful bride : wedding invitations : a stylish bride's guide to simple, handmade
    wedding correspondence / April L. Paffrath and Laura McFadden.
        p.   cm.
    Includes bibliographical references.
    ISBN 1-59253-037-0 (pbk.)
    1. Invitation cards. 2. Weddings. 3. Paper work. I. McFadden, Laura. II. Title.
    TT872.P34 2004

    392.5—dc22   2003023175

ISBN 1-59253-037-0

10 9 8 7 6 5 4 3 2 1

Design: Laura McFadden Design, Inc.
laura.mcfadden@rcn.com
Cover Image: Bobbie Bush Photography
www.bobbiebush.com
All project designs by authors except where noted.

Printed in Singapore

Catharine Smith

and

Anthony Kent

invite you to share their joy

as they unite in marriage

and afterward for a clambake

and dancing in the sand

Saturday, September sixth

one o'clock in the afternoon

on the beach at Lighthouse Resort

Brigantine, New Jersey

Kindly rep...

M _____

will _____

Contents

Announcements, Save-the-Date Cards, Shower Invitations

An Invitation of Your Own

Ever wonder why most wedding invitations look the same? So have we. We think it's a little odd that it can be difficult to distinguish between all the different invitations we've received. Sometimes we would be hard-pressed to match up invitations with the lovely, hip people who sent them. But what's so sad about that, really? Simply that people agonized over the design decisions. Agonized. They had to choose from all the fonts and all the paper choices—not to mention wording—and arrive at an emblematic invitation. Unfortunately, the frequent choices seem adapted more to the popular idea of a wedding than to the style and personality of the couple. It's a shame because there are endless options and variations. The invitation is the first signal to others that a happy event is destined for the near future. Choosing one that fits you, and not every other couple out there, will also make it easier to coordinate other elements in the celebration. (For example, if you choose a violet-colored invitation, you might echo that violet elsewhere. If you choose an elaborate, floral invitation, you can include a design of the same weight and density elsewhere in your preparations.)

With all the amazing materials available, we want you to think creatively. Take some time to create an invitation that reflects you, your style, and the event you're planning. Remember that with so many outrageous and gorgeous papers available, you can choose any of them— you don't have to choose the one that looks the most "wedding-y." Narrow it down to the ones that you think are gorgeous, and take it from there. You can make some-

thing that suits the event and says "you" all over it. The recipients will know immediately that the invitation is from you, or at least one of their more savvy, free-thinking friends.

As pretty as handmade paper with pressed wildflowers can be, it can't suit everyone, so don't try to force that look on yourself. Wildflower paper is beautiful, but it seems like it is used a little too frequently to convince us that *everyone* has chosen it because it fits their style. We should all help out the genuine wildflower people and choose something different that definitely fits. Of course, if you are one of the wildflower paper people at heart, then feel liberated in that choice because the invitation will embody your style completely. And, perhaps now, people will not ride the coattails of your amazing style.

We know you won't choose what works for someone else unless it also fits you just as well. So how to make a good choice? First, realize that there are several options that will fit you very well. You're multi-faceted and your tastes will obviously reflect that. Pay attention to color and texture right off the bat. If you have a gut reaction to a color, hang onto it, even if you can't see how opalescent gray will work into an invitation. When a color strikes you, keep it around and see how it will work with the other textures and colors that you have gathered. Clearly you can't use them all, but part of the creative endeavor is playing with materials and seeing how they can work together to create a look.

Remember to keep it simple. Even an elaborate-looking invitation is a simple combination of materials. Add one too many patterns and the

balance is ruined. Include too many colors and there is no grounding for the design. Layer a few items and see if any element distracts your eye too much. You want enough movement and cooperation between materials, but you want it to be balanced as well.

With that in mind, we've created a collection of intriguing and innovative invitations. You like the color of one and the look of another? Mix them. We're here to brainstorm, to give you different ideas and methods so you can spark your own ideas to life. We know you're tremendously hip and stylish. Get an invitation to match.

We're getting hitched!
Our joy will be more complete
if you celebrate with us.
Nimali Jacobson
&
Hermes Fernands
Saturday, October 6, 2003

4 p.m.

St. Thomas Church
New York, New York

Green and Lovely

SPRINGY, RIBBONED INVITATION

Spring is in the air, in your heart, and in your step. Why not let it show? Go on, spread the green and wrap up this leafy invitation. The layers of different, but coordinating, green create a translucent effect like light filtering through the tree canopy in your neighborhood park. The effect mimics the growth of a new season.

DIRECTIONS

1. Using your favorite page layout program, create a new document 8 ½" × 11" (22 cm × 28 cm).

2. Draw a box 3 ½" wide × 4 ½" deep (9 cm × 11 cm). Set the type for your invitation in the box, leaving about ¾" (2 cm) on top blank for the flower. We used 14 point Bernhard Tango Swash type on leading of 25 points. We chose a coordinating dark green for the type.

3. Once you've perfected the first invitation, copy and paste an additional one right next to the original and two below. This way, you'll be able to run four up on the 8 ½" × 11" (22 cm × 28 cm) sheet.

4. Print onto 8 ½" × 11" (22 cm × 28 cm) scroll cream paper and trim.

5. Center printed scroll paper invite onto ric-rac card. Place a needle through the two cards about ¼" (0.5 cm) down from top of scroll paper and pierce through the two layers.

6. Place flower in through hole and twist the wire around the back in a coil.

7. Draw a rectangle, 9" wide × 5 ¾" deep (23 cm × 14.5 cm), onto sage vellum. Trim paper to size with craft knife.

8. Center assembled invite onto sage rectangle. Fold left side of sage vellum over right so ends meet in the middle. Score edges with bone folder.

9. Wrap with leaf ribbon and insert in chroma lime vellum envelope.

VARIATION *For autumn wedding colors, replace the greens with russet, burnt sienna, orange, and yellow colors.*

MATERIALS

8 ½" × 11" (22 cm × 28 cm) scroll cream paper

4 ¼" × 5 ½" (10.5 cm × 14 cm) A2 butter colored ric-rac cards

heavy-duty embroidery needle

green and yellow silk favor flowers with metal stems

coordinating 2"-wide (5 cm) leaf ribbon

8 ½" × 11" (22 cm × 28 cm) sage-colored vellum

4¾" × 6 ½" (12 cm × 17 cm) chroma lime vellum envelopes

personal computer

page layout software (such as Quark or PageMaker)

color printer

pencil

metal ruler

drafting triangle

craft knife

bone folder

No Two Alike

THUMBPRINT CARD

MATERIALS

11" × 17"
(28 cm × 43 cm) white
cover-weight stock

personal computer

page layout software
(such as Quark or
Page Maker)

color printer

bone folder

craft knife

4 ½" × 6"
(11 cm × 15 cm)
red envelopes

Obviously, you and your intended are stylish and individual. Give your invitations your own personal mark—literally. Of course, you can enlist some friends to help you make these invitations and no one will care if the thumbprints belong to you two or not, unless you have an FBI agent on your guest list. (Would we assume that you don't? Never!) However, it is much more fulfilling and, indeed, sweet to spend a little quality time together when it may be a scarce commodity. Talk about your plans, the red ink you've accidentally smeared across your face, or why the dog loves it when you play bossa nova music. Just cherish the time and know that you have sent an inimitable mark of your union to all of your guests.

DIRECTIONS

1. Using your favorite page layout software, create a document 16" wide × 5 ½" deep (41 cm × 14 cm).

2. Divide the layout into four sections and mark with vertical rules, 4" (10 cm) wide for each section.

3. In the first section, set the type for the first name to appear on the invitation, approximately 3 ¼" (8.5 cm) from the top and centered left to right. We used 9 point Garamond on 13 point leading.

4. Do the same in the second and third sections, setting the type for the second name and subsequent names together accordingly.

5. In the fourth section, set the invitation with all the pertinent information.

TIP *If you are new to the scanning and layout game, have no fear (OK, less fear). You can go a more low-tech, but somewhat messier route, and stamp each invitation with your lovely prints. Technology makes this project swifter, but don't forget that you have the basic tools, literally, at your very fingertips.*

Mr. and Mrs. Donald Albert Boyer
request the honour of your presence
at the Nuptial Mass uniting their daughter

Leeann Marie
and
James Francis Doherty

in the Sacrament of Holy Matrimony
Saturday, the twenty-fifth of September
Nineteen hundred and ninety-nine
at two o'clock in the afternoon
St. Mary's Roman Catholic Church
Charlestown, Massachusetts

6. Remove the vertical lines from the four sections.

7. Place your thumbs on a red inkpad, press stamp onto white paper in the patterns shown, and scan into your computer.

8. Place thumbprint images in document and then print out on a white textured 11" × 17" (28 cm × 43 cm) cover-weight stock. If you don't have a large-format printer, bring it on a disk to a copy center and have them print it.

9. Fold the card into four sections and score with a bone folder.

10. Place in red envelopes.

VARIATION *If you don't own a large-format printer, you could make a small card and attach it into the last panel of the card and handprint the names under the thumbprints.*

Please join us in the
celebration of our love

~

Carlos Santiago
&
Birthe Cruetz

~

Saturday May 29, 2004

4 o'clock p.m.

~

Church of the Transfiguration

West Collingswood, New Jersey

~

Reception to follow

Arts and Crafts Style
VERTICAL ARTISAN INVITATION

William Morris was headed for a life in the church before turning to art and becoming one of the one of the earliest movers and shakers in the Arts and Crafts movement. Elevating craftsmanship to a fine art, Morris worked with a band of talented people, such as Burne-Jones and Rossetti, creating works of all kinds, from furniture to windows to tiles. Morris's most well-known type of creation influenced this design—his intricate and complex wallpapers. A simple invitation on plain paper is wrapped in a swath of detailed floral paper and tied with a coordinating ribbon. This invitation is nested inside an end-opening envelope that makes the most of the vertical orientation—and makes it feel like anything but business.

DIRECTIONS

1. Using your favorite page layout program, create a new document 8 ½" × 11" (22 cm × 28 cm).

2. Draw a box 3 ¾" wide × 9" deep (9.5 cm × 23 cm). Set the type for your invitation in the box, leaving a 1 ¾" (4.5 cm) margin at the top and bottom. (We used 14 point Amphora on leading of 23 points. Color the text dark green.)

3. Once you've perfected the first invitation, copy and paste an additional one right next to the original. This way you'll be able to run two up, side by side on the 8 ½" × 11" (22 cm × 28 cm) sheet.

4. Print the invitations out on the 8 ½" × 11" (22 cm × 28 cm) cream-colored card stock (you may first want to test this out on white printer paper to make sure you like the way it looks).

VARIATION *For a more vibrant look, this can also be made with salmon-colored stock to match the salmon-colored envelopes.*

MATERIALS

4 ⅛" × 9 ⅛" (10.3 cm × 23.3 cm) salmon-colored envelope with flap on long end

8 ½" × 11" (22 cm × 28 cm) coordinating cream-colored cover stock

8 ½" × 11" (22 cm × 28 cm) or larger sheet of decorative paper

deckled edged scissors or rotary paper trimmer with deckled-edge attachment

¼" wide × 15" long (0.5 cm × 38 cm) of coordinating ribbon

personal computer

page layout program (such as Quark or PageMaker)

color printer

triangle

pencil

metal ruler

craft knife

bone folder

scissors

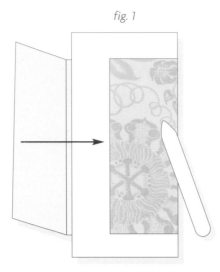

fig. 1

5. Trim the invitation with your rotary cutter or utility knife and ruler.

6. Place a sheet of the decorative paper, face down, on your cutting surface. Draw a rectangle 11" wide × 6" deep (28 cm × 15 cm). Trim paper to size with craft knife.

7. Deckle the edges of the wide side of the paper with rotary trimmer or deckled-edged scissors.

8. Assemble the invitation. Place paper on work surface decorative side down *(see fig. 1)*. Place cream-colored invite face up in center of the wide side of the decorative paper. Fold left over right sides of decorative paper into the center of the invitation and score each side with bone folder.

9. Tie ribbon in a knot and trim excess with scissors.

10. Insert in salmon-colored envelope.

TIP *When using a complex paper pattern, choose your ribbon carefully. You want colors to mesh, but too much detail in the ribbon, like a pattern of its own, steals the oomph of the gorgeous paper you've picked. Save the elaborate ties for use with simple papers.*

SOMETHING
OLD
NEW
BORROWED
&BLUE

PROJECT DESIGN: ANNA HERRICK AND LAURA McFADDEN

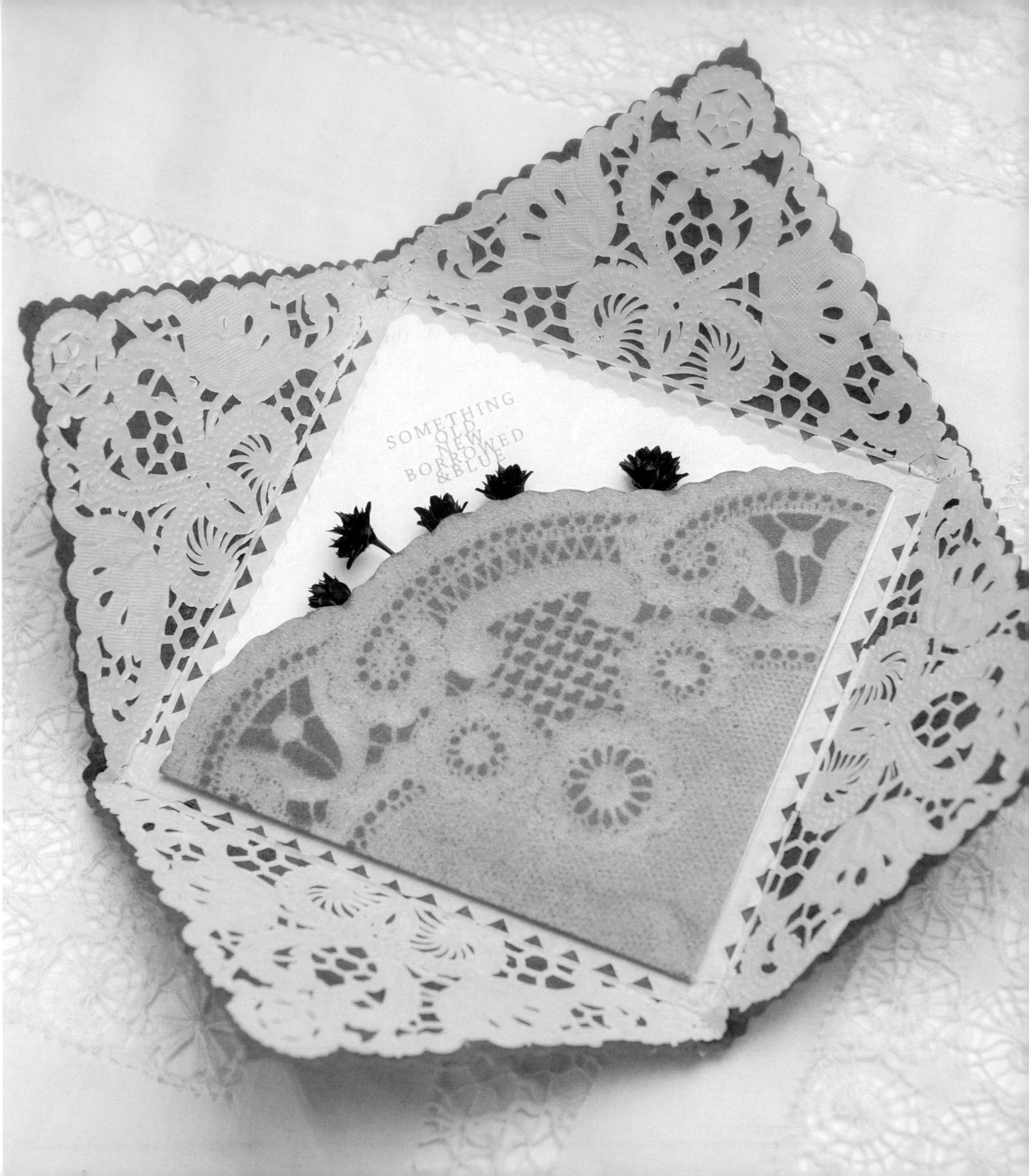

Something Blue
SUN-PRINT LACY INVITE

Who says lace needs to be white and frilly? This lace is blue, baby! Sun prints are made by placing an object on light-sensitive paper. As the sunlight strikes the paper, the lace blocks and leaves its design behind. And while you make the print, you'll be dosing up on vitamin D: essential for energy and good moods (OK, that may or may not be true, but it sure sounds good to us). The diamond shape of this invitation creates a pocket for all the elements of the invitation.

DIRECTIONS FOR THE LACE ENCLOSURE

1. Place sun-print paper on a piece of cardboard and place circular doily on top of sunprint sheet. Expose to sunlight anywhere from 1 to 5 minutes or until the sheet starts to turn white.

2. Rinse sheet with water and let dry. It may take some experimentation to get the print looking the way you want it, so you may want to try doing several at once, pulling them out of the sunlight at different times.

3. Scan the photo into your computer. If this is not an option, bring it to a graphics shop, have them scan it for you and place it onto a disk.

4. Create a document in your layout program 10 ½" wide × 5 ¾" deep (27 cm × 14.5 cm). Place digital image on right side of page and scale up photo until it measures 5 ¼" (13.5 cm) square. Align image on top and right edges.

5. Output image onto white card stock.

VARIATION *If you have difficulty rotating the type on the 45° angle, just set it in the square on the page.*

MATERIALS

Sun-print kit with 4 ¼" (10.5 cm) square sheets

circular doily

scanner

personal computer

page layout program (such as Quark or PageMaker)

color printer

8 ½" × 11" (22 cm × 28 cm) white laser or inkjet card stock

craft knife

metal ruler

triangle

bone folder

craft glue

Obonai white laser or inkjet rice paper

spray adhesive

small blue dried flowers

thin gauge wire

scalloped paper edgers or rotary trimmer with scalloped-edge rotary blade

scissors

8" × 8" (20 cm × 20 cm) white paper doilies

sheet of decorative blue paper cut down to 8 ¼" (20.5 cm) square

daisy wafer seals

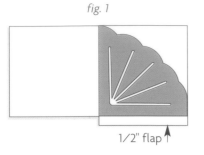

fig. 1

1/2" flap ↑

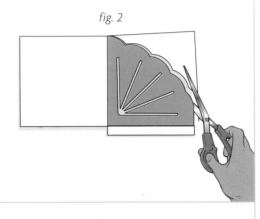

fig. 2

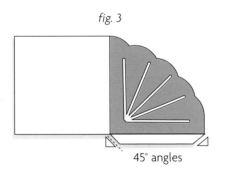

fig. 3

45° angles

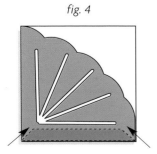

fig. 4

6. Trim image to size leaving a ½" (1 cm) flap under the image side of the printed card *(see fig. 1)*.

7. Using scissors or craft knife, cut around shape of doily *(see fig. 2)*.

8. Cut 45° angles in on flap as shown *(see fig. 3)*.

9. Fold card in half and burnish with bone folder. Reopen card and fold left square half behind scalloped half.

10. Using craft glue, adhere the ½" (1 cm) flap to inside back of card *(see fig. 4)*.

DIRECTIONS FOR THE INVITATION, DIRECTIONS, AND RSVP PAGES

1. Create a new document 4 ¾" (11.5 cm) square.

2. Set the type for your invitation and rotate text on a 45° angle (*we used 8 point Chaparral Display type on leading of 13 points*).

3. Create a new page and set the type for your directions, rotating text on a 45° angle as well.

4. Create another new page and set the type for your RSVP, also rotating that text.

5. Print out invitation and directions onto the Obanai white laser paper and set aside.

6. Print the RSVP onto the white laser card stock.

7. Trim all edges of each page with scalloped paper edgers or rotary trimmer.

8. Place a postcard stamp on your RSVP card and handwrite your return address on it.

9. Stuff enclosure with all four sheets.

10. Fan out five dried flowers and join together at base by wrapping a piece of wire at base of bouquet.

11. Place dried flowers in enclosure.

DIRECTIONS FOR THE ENVELOPE

SOMETHING
OLD
NEW
BORROWED
&BLUE

1. Cut out an 8 ½" (22 cm) square of the decorative blue paper.

2. Spray adhesive on the back of one of the 8" (20 cm) square doilies and adhere to the blue paper.

3. Trim edges of the blue paper with the scalloped paper edgers or rotary trimmer with the scalloped attachment.

4. Fold in edges of lace doily and burnish edges with the bone folder.

5. Glue three edges with craft glue.

6. Place enclosure into envelope and seal with a daisy sticker.

7. Address the envelope with a white gel marker.

Curvy Embrace

INTERLOCKING ENCLOSURE

The inspiration for this invitation comes from a hefty, lovely purchase on Madison Avenue (of course). Actually, the purchase itself was weighty crystal, but the real spark of this idea came from the receipt. That's right. Sometimes, swanky *objets* at high-end boutiques result in elaborate proofs of purchase (who wants to look at paper from a register when there are goodies in the bag, for heaven's sake?). Their lovely receipt enclosure was quite different from this invitation, but the idea is the same: curvy forms of paper that interlock to cradle the enclosed paper. We used chocolate brown and violet to mimic the lovely window display in a pâtisserie.

DIRECTIONS

1. Cut two 5" × 11" (13 cm × 28 cm) pieces of cover-weight paper.

2. Cover 5" (13 cm) of one end of each piece of paper with spray adhesive. Align the sprayed sections of the papers and firmly press together so that the pieces overlap exactly 5" (13 cm), making a long, thin strip.

3. Using the bone folder, score the paper at each edge of the 5" (13 cm) overlap. Enlarge the template from page 77 to 200 percent. Align the template with the scored edges. Cut along the template guide, making sure to cut in far enough where the circles meet (the cut should extend just past a point 2 ½" (6 cm) from the scored line).

4. Fold the flaps inward on the score line, using a bone folder to make the folded edges crisp.

5. Using your computer, create a 4 ⅛" (12 cm) document and set your invitation wording. We used 10 point Colonna MT text on leading of 22 points. Coordinate your font color with enclosure colors. Print document onto blue card-weight paper. Trim the invitation document using scalloped edge of rotary trimmer or scalloped paper edger scissors.

6. Use a small amount of glue at the top of enclosure and adhere the invitation paper. Interlock the circles to close the invitation.

7. Tie a coordinating ribbon around the finished invitation enclosure.

VARIATION *For more contrast between the interlocking panels, use two colors for the enclosure instead of one.*

MATERIALS

8 ½" × 11" (22 cm × 28 cm) brown stardream cover weight paper

8 ½" × 11" (22 cm × 28 cm) blue card stock

scissors

paper cutter

rotary trimmer with scalloped-edge blade or paper edger scissors

bone folder

spray adhesive

glue stick

personal computer

page layout software (such as Quark or PageMaker)

color printer

template from page 77

12" (30 cm) length of blue silk ribbon

"Princely" Frog Invite

ASIAN-STYLE FROG ENCLOSURE

MATERIALS

20" × 28"
(51 cm × 71 cm)
decorative
Chinese-style paper

5" (13 cm) square
white petal envelope

red Chinese
frog closure

salmon-colored laser
or inkjet card stock

spray adhesive

craft knife

metal ruler

sewing needle

red thread

bone folder

personal computer

page layout software
(such as Quark or
PageMaker)

color printer

Small pieces of gorgeous paper and some braided frogs (those twisted pieces of shiny cord) are all you need to transform a simple petal envelope into a classic and elegant invitation enclosure. Choose coordinating paper and frogs, but don't go too matchy-matchy; contrast within the realm of coordination will make the frog stand out. When finished, this invitation makes a dazzling impression of sophistication; so if you're secretly hoping to keep attendance numbers down, don't send this invitation—people won't be able to resist the event that goes with this card.

This invitation is a great way to use the wide array of handprinted, or otherwise gorgeous, papers. Why decide on just one pattern? Use the papers that appeal to you and avoid the difficult decision of choosing just one.

DIRECTIONS FOR THE ENCLOSURE ENVELOPE

1. Place the Chinese paper decorative side down on your work surface and cut it down to 12" (30 cm) square.

2. Spray adhesive on the nondecorative side of the paper and adhere to the front of the petal envelope. Burnish entire surface by rubbing the bone folder across the surface several times.

3. Trim around petal edges with craft knife *(see fig. 1)*. Cut off two of the petals *(see fig. 2)* and put aside. Fold in remaining petals and burnish to make edges crisp.

TIP *You can make several layers to go into the enclosure. Make an RSVP card and a directions card and output onto the salmon-colored card stock.*

fig. 1

fig. 2

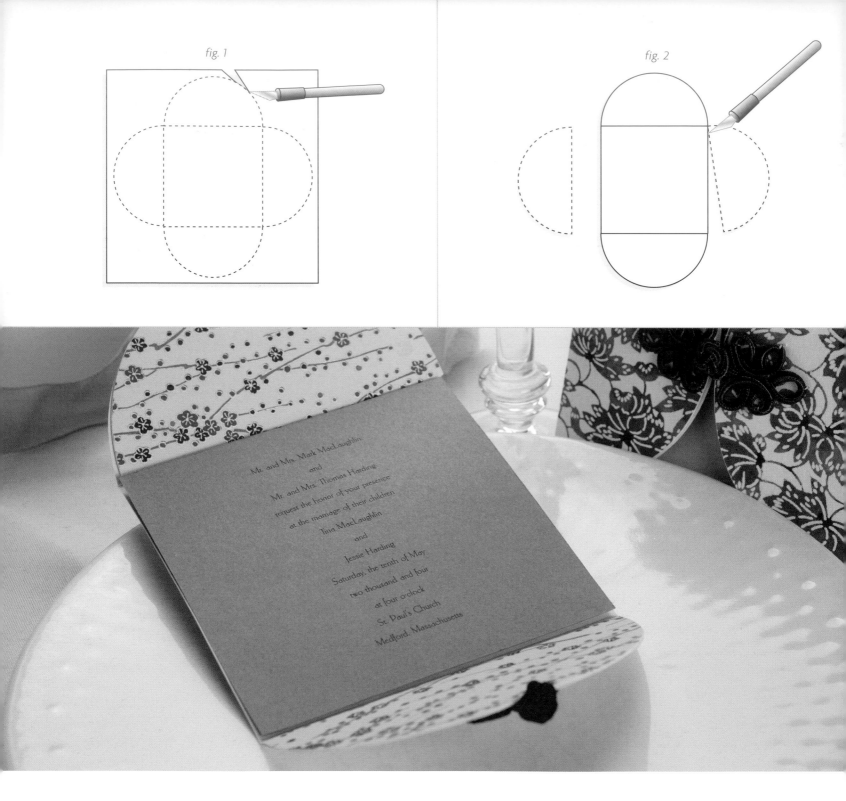

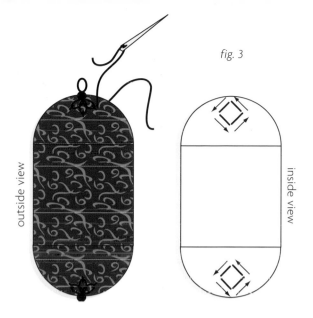

fig. 3

outside view

inside view

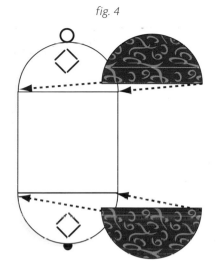

fig. 4

4. Sew frogs onto the front top and bottoms of the petal envelope *(see fig. 3)*, stitching in and out from plain to decorative sides of envelope.

5. Open enclosure and place decorative side down on your work surface.

6. Spray adhesive onto nondecorative side of the petals that had previously been put aside. Adhere petals to inside of enclosure, covering the nondecorative side with the sewn petals *(see fig. 4)*.

7. Cut any excess overlap away around petal shape.

DIRECTIONS FOR THE INVITATION

1. Create a new document in your page layout software that is 5 $\frac{1}{4}$" (13.5 cm) square.

2. Set the text for your invitation (we used 12 point Carlton Letter on leading of 22 points).

3. Print out onto salmon-colored card stock and trim so edges are flush with edges of closure.

4. Place into envelope.

VARIATION *If the petals do not cover your typography, consider making an invitation that folds in half with a blank cover and fits inside the petal enclosure.*

What the Buzz Is About

DRAGONFLY POP-UP INVITATION

MATERIALS

2 sheets 8 ½" × 11"
(22 cm × 28 cm)
lavender card stock

36" (91 cm) -long pieces
of organdy ribbon
in lavender,
pale green, and gold

1 piece 8 ½" × 11"
(22 cm × 28 cm) pale
green vellum

1 piece 8 ½" × 11"
(22 cm × 28 cm)
gold vellum

dragonfly stamp

stamping inks in
green and gold

gold marker

2 head pins

2 tiny blue beads

2 tiny
turquoise beads

wire cutters

craft knife

6" × 8 ³/4"
(15 cm × 22.5 cm)
envelope

¹/8"-wide (.3 cm)
double-sided tape

PVA glue

The dragonfly, with its opalescent colors and diaphanous wings, has long been a staple of art and folklore. Throughout the world, the dragonfly represents a plethora of characteristics, from mischief-maker to symbol of happiness and strength. For this particular purpose, we're partial to the Native American Zuni tale of the helpful dragonfly who became an important messenger. In this invitation he is a messenger of great news. Whatever the symbology, the long lines of the dragonfly recall the easy days at the height of summer. The purple and green tones echo an earthy, natural attitude and simplicity.

DIRECTIONS FOR INVITATION

1. Fold an 11"-wide × 8 ½"-high (28 cm × 22 cm) lavender card stock in half vertically, using a bone folder to make a neat fold.

2. From another piece of lavender card stock, cut a rectangle 4" wide × 1 ½" high (11 cm × 4 cm). Fold in half vertically away from you to make a "mountain" crease, unfold, then measure ½" (1 cm) from each end and fold under (you should have a ½" by 1 ½" (1 cm × 4 cm) piece folded under).

3. Inside the 11" × 8 ½" (28 cm × 22 cm) card, mark a spot 4" (10 cm) from the left and right sides of the card and using double-sided tape, attach the two folded-under edges to the card, with crease centered, and centered from top to bottom. Crease should form a "mountain" to the "valley" formed by the card itself when the invitation is closed a little bit *(see fig. 1 on page 30)*.

VARIATION *The dragonfly was once the symbol of Japan, "the dragonfly island." Evoke that symbolism by shifting your color scheme slightly to white, black, and crimson.*

Katherine Winters
and
Gregory Gibeault
would be delighted
to have you share
in the joy of their marriage
Saturday, the fifth of July
at half after four o'clock
and afterward for dinner
and dancing under the stars
Oakleaf Arboretum
French Creek, Pennsylvania

Kindly reply by the fifth of June
M_____
will_____attend the wedding

PROJECT DESIGN: ANDREA RENZI MCFADDEN

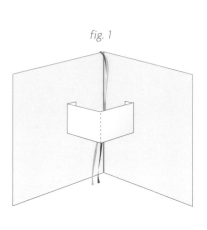

fig. 1

4. On scraps of lavender card stock, lightly tap or drag your stamp pad to add a green ink glaze. Let dry, then stamp two dragonflies with gold ink. Let dry and then use craft knife to cut out.

5. Put a dab of glue on each bead, and thread one bead onto each head pin. Trim pins with wire cutters so they are only ½" (1 cm) long. Use glue to attach pins to back of each dragonfly, so that only "eyes" show from the front. When glue is dry, crease dragonfly wings slightly to imitate real wings. Use double-sided tape to attach one to each side of the creased pop-up. Place them so they look as though they are about to kiss!

6. On an 11" wide × 8 ½" high (28 cm × 22 cm) piece of paper, print your invitation so that it appears on the left 5 ½" × 8 ½" (14 cm × 22 cm) panel in landscape view. Crease in half vertically. Using a pencil, draw a light line ¼" (.5 cm) from right side, and using the line as a guide, trim the right edge of the paper with scalloped craft scissors. Line the trimmed edge with the gold marker.

7. Crease a piece of pale green 11" wide × 8 ½" high (28 cm × 22 cm) vellum in half vertically. Using a pencil, draw a light line ½" (1 cm) from right side, and using the line as a guide, trim the right edge of the paper with scalloped craft scissors.

8. Line up three pieces of ribbon. Pull all three through the "tunnel" formed by the pop-up in the card and then lay the card pop-up down on the table. Put the invitation on, then layer the vellum. Bring ribbons together and tie in a bow to hold layers together. Stamp a few gold dragonflies on vellum around the invitation. Let dry. On inside of card, stamp more dragonflies in gold and green flying around the page. You can also make some look like they are flying off the edge.

9. Line the envelope with a piece of gold vellum trimmed to fit. Stamp dragonflies randomly on return envelope, avoiding areas for addressing.

DIRECTIONS FOR RSVP CARD

1. Print "RSVP" on 5 ½" wide × 4" high (14 cm × 10 cm) lavender paper. Using a pencil, draw a light line ¼" (0.5 cm) from bottom edge, and using the line as a guide, trim the right edge of the paper with scalloped craft scissors.

2. Stamp two dragonflies. Line the trimmed edge with the gold marker. Attach with double-edged tape to card stock. Stamp dragonflies randomly on return envelope, avoiding the address area.

RSVP MATERIALS

5 1/2" wide × 4" high (14 cm × 10 cm) lavender card stock

envelope

dragonfly stamp

stamping inks in green and gold

gold marker

4 1/4" × 5" (10.5 cm × 13 cm) envelope

It's Not Your Whole Life

KEEPING THINGS IN PERSPECTIVE

Obviously, we think that the world of invitations holds great promise—after all, we've written a book all about those nuptial missives. Because we are thrilled by the potential creativity invitations offer, we are well aware of how consuming they can be. Add to that the cultural tendency to dive head-first into wedding planning without checking the water depth and you have the makings of energy deflation, frustration, and inundation. Not good. You deserve much better (and so does everyone around you).

Take it all in perspective. A wedding is a fabulous thing—and we do mean fabulous—but a life is even better. A wedding is a prelude to a marriage, after all, and the second part is more important. Don't get caught up in ceremonial details and forsake all that has made you stylish, savvy, and inimitable all along.

Throwing a gigantic party can be intimidating, and it's somewhat normal to obsess about the direction of the event and the details that make it stand out. Most engagements last from six months to one year. When is the last time you spent ten months planning a party? True, you probably want it to be quite a bit more special than your Friday evening progressive cocktail parties, but that does not mean that every moment of the many months until the happy event needs to be filled with plans, ideas, and conversations about it. You should be able to fall asleep at night thinking about something besides "the big day." It may take a little bit of work, but teach yourself how to incorporate the planning into your normal life. Wedding planning is not a hobby, and it would be a shame to replace your usual activities, nights out, parties, and yoga classes completely with a world of typefaces, color schemes, and guest lists.

It may be difficult when your loved ones want to hear the latest incarnation of your plans. But it is essential to keep your wits and wittiness about you. Keep in mind that your wedding takes up a single day in your life—or an entire weekend at the most. After it is over, you have the rest of your life ahead. Can you bear to have spent every conversation and waking moment thinking about this one day, with no thought to the weeks and months after? We didn't think so. And it's not your fault if you slide in that direction. We live in a culture where the planning of a wedding gets inflated monumentally, and that's a lot of pressure for one single day to handle. Have fun with the planning and the conversations, but mix it into your regular existence and your usual personality. Share your excitement with people, but remember to leave yourself room to get excited about other things as well.

If you get stuck in a wedding whirlpool, try the following:

- Have a discussion about the state of politics in some town, state, or country (as you once did before you started planning).

- Go shopping for shoes and makeup that you won't be wearing on your wedding day.

- Plan a non-honeymoon vacation with your soon-to-be-spouse that will take place three months after you get married.

- Institute a "wedding talk" jar. When you need a break from the pressures and constancy of planning, put a quarter in the jar for each time you infringe on your own limits.

- Tell friends who won't let the subject drop that you love that they are excited, but you need to talk about regular stuff for a bit.

Invitations are one of the first items to be tackled when planning a wedding. Because they set the tone for the event to come and give guests a first glimpse of what lies ahead, they can be a major drain on the amount of energy you've allotted to wedding planning. That's why we've tried to come up with many ideas to spur your own creativity and help you maximize your time and efforts. Invitation planning and production can be enjoyable, relaxing, rewarding, and even a little meditative. However, it can just as easily turn into an indecision fest where papers, fonts, and colors confuse you. Take it easy. Make a simple plan, and have fun with your creation. Learn when to let something go. Making an invitation design overly complex will result in an unfocused piece that has no style or impact. Go for a reflection of your own personalities and let it stop there. And in the end, as important as an invitation's role is in the whole process, it isn't the most important thing. What you two feel like after the wedding weighs a lot more heavily on that scale.

Bride in a Can

SPRINGY BRIDAL SURPRISE

Sometimes, a wedding invitation is a surprise. This one *really* is. Remember the joke can of salted nuts that really held coiled spring snakes to shock unsuspecting friends? This invitation works on the same idea. The reference to the old joke as well as the quirky humor makes this invitation a gem.

DIRECTIONS FOR BRIDE

1. Place the 3" (8 cm) piece of cardboard under the bottom of the spring and trace around the shape to form a circle.

2. Cut out the cardboard circle.

3. Cut a 4" (10 cm) square of tulle.

4. Fold the tulle in half. Then place the cardboard into the center of the tulle as shown *(see fig. 1 on page 36)*.

5. Place tulle and cardboard composite into the second coil of the spring *(see fig. 2)* and sew to spring parameter.

6. Cut a rectangle of cotton fabric measuring 20" long × 2 ½" wide (51 cm × 6 cm).

7. Fold fabric in half vertically.

8. Iron fabric and pin sides as shown *(see fig. 3)*.

9. Create a sheath by sewing seams ¼" (0.5 cm) in on pinned sides and turn right-side out, keeping sewn seams inside. One end should be left completely open.

10. Iron flat.

VARIATION *You could also use this for a bridal shower invitation or a card to give to a bride and groom.*

MATERIALS

3" (8 cm) square piece of cardboard

pencil

scissors

cupcake topper bride

6" long × 2 ¼" wide (15 cm × 5.5 cm) aluminum bottle

dismantled "snake in a can" spring

5" wide (13 cm) tulle ribbon

sewing needle

white sewing thread

small silk flower

¼" (0.5 cm) pink rhinestone (optional)

¼ yard (0.23 m) lightweight white cotton fabric

sewing machine

iron

personal computer

page layout software (such as Quark or PageMaker)

pearlescent printer paper

printer

decorative paper

craft knife

metal ruler

craft glue

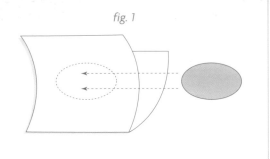

fig. 1

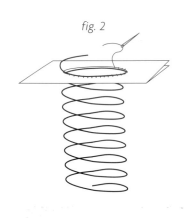

fig. 3

fig. 2

11. Place spring inside sheath, leaving sewn cardboard and tulle composite closest to open end of sheath *(see fig. 4)*.

12. Place cupcake bride into the center of the coil, so she stands on tulle and cardboard composite. Make sure seam of sheath is lined up with her back.

13. Tuck in frayed edges of fabric around top.

14. Double thread needle with about a 12-inch (30 cm) length of white thread and tie a knot at the end. Starting at seam of sheath, baste around the top of the sheath going in and out through tucked-over edge and exterior edge and pull tight to form a gather around bride's waist *(see fig. 5)*.

15. Secure skirt onto bride by sewing around holes in her arms.

16. Tie a knot at back of sheath, which is now her skirt.

17. Cut out a 5" × 8" (13 cm × 20 cm) rectangle of tulle and repeat steps 13 and 14 to form second layer of dress.

18. Tie a silk flower around her waist and secure wire around flower.

fig. 4

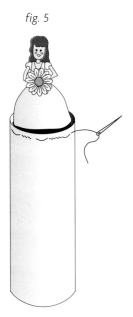

fig. 5

DIRECTIONS FOR RSVP

1. Using your favorite page layout program, create a document 10" wide × 4" deep (25 cm × 10 cm). Create a light pink box with a ¼" (0.5 cm) border of white all around.

2. Draw a dotted vertical line 5" (13 cm) from left edge. Insert the scissors character from the Zapf Dingbat font along the dotted line and set the text "cut along fold line and mail back postcard" going up the side of the line.

3. Scan template for corners (shown right) as a .tiff at 100 percent and paste them into your document at corners of pink box as accents.

4. Create a 65 percent black block 2 ¼" × 4" (5.5 cm × 10 cm) and set wedding invitation in center in white type (we used 7 point Eurostile on leading of 22 points). Center it in the 5-inch wide (13 cm) space.

5. Set "RSVP" on the right side of the card as shown in photo (ours is 6 point Eurostile on leading of 22 points).

6. Print and trim invite.

7. Cut out a 10" × 4" (25 cm × 10 cm) piece of decorative paper.

8. Spray adhere back of 10" × 4" (25 cm × 10 cm) printed invite to wrong side of 10" × 4" (25 cm × 10 cm) decorative paper.

9. Fold in half.

10. For RSVP, create a label to write the address on the decorative side. Either handwrite name or use Avery label system.

*template for
decorative corners*

VARIATION *The aluminum cans may get expensive. A cheaper alternative is a cardboard mailing tube.*

HOW DO I LOVE THEE?

LET ME COUNT THE WAYS

—*Elizabeth Barrett Browning*

Count Us In

ABACUS CARD

The light rattle of this elegant and poetic invitation gives people advance notice of something special as they open the envelope. This invitation is inspired by an abacus necklace engraved with the first words of Elizabeth Barrett Browning's evocative and love-filled poem. That necklace was given decades ago from a thoughtful man to his wife (Laura's father to her mother) and sweetly connects the traditional Chinese counting instrument with one of the best-loved poems in the English language. Here's a twist on that idea.

DIRECTIONS FOR CARD

1. With your favorite page layout software, create a 3 ¾" wide × 5 ½" deep (9.5 cm × 14 cm) document.

2. Draw a window 1" wide × ¾" deep (3 cm × 2 cm). Center horizontally on page and 1 ½" (4 cm) from top of page.

3. Set type under box "How do I love thee? Let me count the ways."—*Elizabeth Barrett Browning*. Quote is set in 8 point Scala caps type on leading of 17 points. Author's name is 8 point Scala Italic. Type color: 60 percent black.

4. Print document onto 8 ½" × 11" (22 cm × 28 cm) pearlescent cover stock and trim.

5. Using decorative paper, draw and cut out two rectangles 9" wide × 6 ¼" deep (23 cm × 15.5 cm).

6. Spray mount two sides together, decorative sides facing out, and fold in half width-wise, using a bone folder to score the edges.

7. Spray mount printed pearlescent sheet to front of card, centering within decorative rectangle.

8. Unfold and lay card flat facing up and cut out window.

MATERIALS

8 ½" × 11" (22 cm × 20 cm) pearlescent cover stock

8 ½" × 11" (22 cm × 28 cm), or larger, sheet decorative paper

three 2"-long (5 cm) dressmaker's pins

adhesive tape

repositionable spray mount adhesive

personal computer

page layout program (such as Quark or PageMaker)

color printer

triangle

pencil

metal ruler

craft knife

bone folder

silver-colored seed beads

4 ¾" × 6 ½" (12 cm × 17 cm) pearlescent envelope

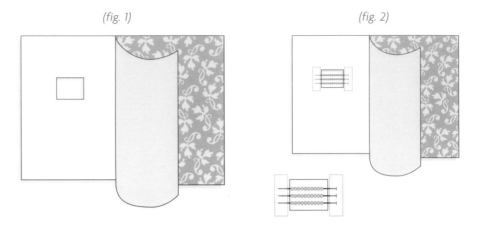

(fig. 1)

(fig. 2)

9. Flip card over so inside spread faces up. Temporarily pull apart the two decorative paper layers on left side of the card *(see fig. 1)*.

10. Take three straight pins and gather up ten seed beads onto each pin.

11. Place and center horizontally in cut-out window. Tape sides of pins to back of card and reposition decorative paper back over left hand side of the card *(see fig. 2)*.

12. Burnish with bone folder until all of the air bubbles have disappeared.

DIRECTIONS FOR INVITATION INSERT

1. With your favorite page layout software, create a new document 4 ½" wide × 6 ¼" deep (11 cm × 15.5 cm).

2. Set invitation type. Type should start roughly 3" (8 cm) down from top of page. Ours is set as follows: 8 point Scala caps on leading of 17 points. Type color: 60 percent black.

3. Print out on pearlescent paper and trim.

4. Insert in center of card.

5. Insert card in pearlescent envelope.

VARIATION *For a more translucent look, the invitation insert can also be printed on vellum (shown right), which comes in either laser or inkjet varieties. For best results, make sure the vellum matches your printer type.*

ELLEN BARNETT

TO

KEVIN MILLER

JUNE 15, 2004

2 O'CLOCK IN THE AFTERNOON

* * *

SAINT PATRICK'S CATHEDRAL

NEW YORK, NEW YORK

* * *

RECEPTION TO FOLLOW

Bottle of Bliss

INVITATION DESERT-ISLE STYLE

MATERIALS

½ tablespoon sand

flexible bead needle

24" (61 cm) turquoise
embroidery floss

scissors

one ¾" (2 cm)
seashell

several tiny seashells,
beach glass, and
small crystal beads

bottle
7" × 1⅛" × 1⅛"
(18 cm × 4 cm × 4 cm)

one cork

craft glue

4 small
pearl beads

4 seashells with
holes drilled

4 medium
fish beads

6 small
crystal beads

6 tiny
blue beads

8 tiny
turquoise beads

4 medium
blue beads

2 medium
turquoise beads

No, you're not stranded anywhere. Far from it. This beaded bottle stuffed with a coiled invitation evokes the feeling of a tropical paradise. It works perfectly with a beach wedding . . . think casual linens for the entire wedding party, bare feet or sandals you kick off at the kiss. Let people know what kind of festivity they're in for with this carefree approach. After all, there is no one else you'd rather be on a desert isle with than the one you're marrying. This invitation is a way to embody that idea.

DIRECTIONS FOR BOTTLE

1. Pour about ½ tablespoon of sand into the bottle. Add several tiny seashells, pieces of beach glass, crystal beads, or other beach findings to the bottle.

2. Glue the ¾" (2 cm) seashell to the top of the cork.

3. Construct the pull-cord for the invitation: Measure approximately 24" (61 cm) of turquoise embroidery floss. Using a flexible beading needle, thread beads on in the following order: 1 seashell, 1 small pearl, 1 medium blue bead, 3 tiny blue beads, 1 medium fish bead, 1 small crystal bead, 1 tiny turquoise bead, 1 small crystal bead, 1 tiny turquoise bead, 1 small crystal bead, 1 tiny turquoise bead, 1 medium blue bead, 1 small pearl bead, 1 seashell, 1 medium turquoise bead, 1 tiny turquoise bead.

4. At last bead, bring needle and floss through the hole in the tiny bead, then bring it around the outside of the tiny bead and back up through the medium turquoise bead.

5. Tie the floss off to the floss that is going down through the bead, pull, knot tie, and trim closely. Repeat beading process at other end of floss.

TIP *Make sure your shell sticker is large enough to hold all the layers together, otherwise the invitation may be difficult to pry from the mouth of the bottle.*

Catherine Smith

and

Anthony Renzi

invite you to share their joy

as they unite in marriage

and afterward for a clambake

and dancing in the sand

Saturday, September sixth

one o'clock in the afternoon

on the beach at Lighthouse Resort

Brigantine, New Jersey

Kindly rep...

M _____

will _____

PROJECT DESIGN: ANDREA RENZI McFADDEN

MATERIALS FOR INVITATION

1 seashell sticker

paper and vellum in shades of pale blue and turquoise

mailing tube—
2" × 12"
(5 cm × 30 cm)

bubble wrap

wave-pattern paper-edger scissors

double-sided tape

DIRECTIONS FOR INVITATION

1. Typeset then print your invitation on text weight paper (Don't use card stock, it will be too thick to roll tightly enough to fit in the bottle).

2. Print invitation landscape: Make two columns, center invitation in each column, or use best method for your computer so you can fit two on a page.

3. Trim to 5 ½" wide by 7" long (14 cm × 18 cm), using wave pattern craft scissors to trim bottom.

4. Cut a piece of turquoise vellum 5 ½" wide by 7 ¼" long (14 cm × 18.5 cm), using wave-pattern paper-edger scissors to trim bottom.

5. Cut a piece of pale blue vellum 5 ½" wide by 6 ¾" long (14 cm × 17.5 cm), and then use craft scissors with wave pattern to trim bottom off.

6. Stack the invitation, first turquoise vellum, then invitation, then pale vellum, so you can see the graduating wave pattern. Use double-sided tape at the top between the layers to hold together.

7. Lay the invitation out, printed side up. Place the pull cord across it, parallel with the side with the scalloped edge, so that about 5" (13 cm) hangs over one side of the invitation, and roll the invitation tightly enough for it to fit in the bottle. Use a seashell sticker to secure the invitation to itself. Take the long end of the pull cord and bring it over to meet the other end. Then place the invitation in the bottle with the beading hanging out. Put the cork in the bottle.

DIRECTIONS FOR RSVP

1. Print "RSVP" 5 ¼" wide × 4" high (13.2 cm × 10 cm) in upper third of page.

2. Cut pale blue vellum 5 ½" wide × 1 ½" high (14 cm × 4 cm).

3. Cut turquoise vellum 5 ½" wide × 1 ¼" high (14 cm × 3.5 cm).

4. Trim the top of each piece of vellum with the wave-pattern paper-edger scissors. Attach the pale blue then the turquoise vellum to the bottom portion of the RSVP card with double-sided tape. Put one or more seashell stickers on the reply envelope for decoration.

5. Wrap your RSVP around the bottle, wrap with a layer of bubble wrap, and put in mailing tube for shipping.

VARIATION *Place some other fun small items in the bottle, like a pair of miniature flip-flops, sunglasses or bride-and-groom cupcake decorations.*

MATERIALS FOR RSVP

card stock

turquoise vellum

pale blue vellum

5 ½" × 4" (14 cm × 10 cm) envelope

wave-pattern paper-edger scissors

seashell stickers

double-sided tape

marriage

i do

joy

passion

pebble beach country club

party

pebble beach, california.

family

henning thormaelen

forever

groom

lynne g. waring

happiness

march 3, 2004

bride

friends

2 p.m. in the afternoon

love

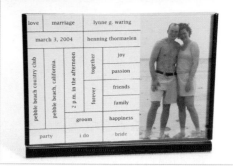

Magnetic Couple
POETRY KIT

Is your love a poem that is rewritten every day? Do your feelings for each other run so deep you're weak in the knees and your thoughts are a jumble? No matter how you rearrange these words, they spell out one thing: great, witty wedding ahead. The pop culture reference that this invitation is based on begs people to play well before they even arrive at the big shindig. Find your guests' not-so-inner Shakespeare. Include instructions, if you think friends won't get the idea right off the bat (your Great-Aunt Hazel might have missed the magnetic poetry craze, after all).

DIRECTIONS

1. In your page layout program, create a new document 11" wide × 8 ½" deep (28 cm × 22 cm).

2. Create a box 5" wide × 3 ½" deep (13 cm × 9 cm).

3. Place digital bride-and-groom photo in page on the right side of the box (ours measures 2" wide × 3 ½" tall (5 cm × 9 cm)).

4. In the same 5" wide × 3 ½" tall (13 cm × 9 cm) box, set type for invitation, dividing words with black rules (we used 9 point Lucida Fax type). Set some of the type horizontally and some vertically to make it look like a game board (see photo above right).

5. Once you've decided on a grid and design you like, copy the box and its graphic elements three times. Set them up on the page 2 across and 2 down.

6. Print out onto an 8 ½" × 11" (22 cm × 28 cm) Avery (or comparable brand) magnet sheet and trim exterior edges.

7. Place onto steel board (optional).

TIP *Create a "How to Play the Game" instruction booklet for the guests. Tell them to cut out the invitation words and place them on their refrigerator doors or the steel game board.*

MATERIALS

digitized photo of
the bride and groom

8 ½" × 11" (22 cm × 28 cm)
Avery magnet sheets

personal computer

scanner

color printer

page layout software
(such as Quark or
PageMaker)

metal ruler

craft knife

4" × 6" (10 cm × 15 cm)
steel board (optional)

All Zipped Up and Ready

ZIPPER-PULL PHOTO INVITATION

Two halves join together to become one entirely neat invitation. Print your picture on one side, your sweetheart's photo on the other, and sew on a zipper. Instead of sending an invitation that just sits there, yours can have moveable parts! You need not have latent punk rock tendencies or a pedigree in the fashion industry to use this invitation to great effect. The invitation card sits inside the zippered enclosure, waiting to be uncovered.

ZIPPER ENCLOSURE DIRECTIONS

1. Create a document in your page layout program 6 1/4" wide × 7 1/8" deep (15.5 cm × 18.3 cm).

2. Import the digital photo into document and enlarge to fill the page.

3. Create a black strip down the center of the page 1/2" wide × 7 1/8" deep (1 cm × 18.3 cm).

4. Print out page onto glossy photo paper and trim to size, also trimming center strip *(see fig. 1 on page 50)*.

5. Place photos about 1/8" (.3 cm) to left and right sides of zipper and glue with the craft glue. Let it set for about 10 minutes.

6. Sew left and right sides of photo with red thread on sewing machine. Use the zipper foot on a sewing machine to get as close as you can to the zipper edge.

7. Cut out a rectangle of the black card stock 11 3/4" wide × 7 1/4" deep (29.3 cm × 18.5 cm).

VARIATION *Fond of your campground courtship? Change the tag on the lanyard of the zipper. Or replace the pull tab with something else: a yin-yang symbol, a heart, a wedding bell, or your initials on a tag.*

MATERIALS

black card stock

digital photo of bride and groom

7" (18 cm) red zipper

glossy photo paper for printers

personal computer

scanner

page layout software (such as Quark or PageMaker)

color printer

sewing machine

craft knife

craft glue

metal ruler

glue stick

wavy red cardboard

white text-weight paper for printers

red thread

bone folder

pencil

scissors

3 mm eyelet grommets

eyelet setting tool

7" wide × 8" deep (18 cm × 20 cm) red envelope

3 ½" wide × 5" deep (9 cm × 13 cm) red envelope

(fig. 1)

(fig. 2)

(fig. 3)

8. Draw pencil lines 2 ¾" (6.5 cm) in from ends of wide side of the paper *(see fig. 2)*.

9. Fold in at pencil lines and burnish with a bone folder at fold.

10. Use a glue stick to adhere front to backing as shown *(see fig. 3)*.

INVITATION INSERT DIRECTIONS

1. Create a document in your page layout program 5 ⅛" wide × 5 ¾" deep (13.3 cm × 14.5 cm).

2. Set type for invitation (we used 11 point AgencyFB-Light Wide on leading of 24 points. We set the red squares in 7 point Zapf Dingbats, letter "n" on leading of 24 points.)

3. Output from printer onto a sheet of the white text weight paper and trim.

4. Cut out a sheet of wavy red card stock 6" wide × 6 ¾" deep (15 cm × 17.5 cm).

5. Place printed white invitation on top of wavy red card stock and center.

6. Punch a hole through the two layers centering it left to right and 1" (3 cm) from the top of the wavy card stock.

7. Place silver grommet in hole and set with eyelet setting tool.

8. Insert invitation into zipper enclosure.

9. Slip into large red envelope.

RSVP DIRECTIONS

1. Create a document in your page layout program 4" wide × 2 ½" deep (10 cm × 6 cm).

2. Set type for "RSVP."

3. Print onto a sheet of the white text-weight paper and trim.

4. Cut out a sheet of wavy red card stock 4 ½" wide × 3" deep (11 cm × 8 cm).

5. Place printed white invitation on top of wavy red card stock and center.

6. Punch a hole through the two layers centering it left to right and 1" (3 cm) from the top of the wavy card stock.

7. Insert silver grommet in hole and set with eyelet setting tool.

8. Slip into small red envelope, stamp red envelope, and handwrite your address.

9. Place in larger red envelope behind invitation.

Swatch Us Get Hitched
PANTONE-STYLE INVITE

This invitation is based on the Pantone swatch booklets that designers use. Some people may not recognize it, but that doesn't diminish the intrigue of the off-center-pivoting, elongated invite. Sleek and contained within the envelope, it splays out to show all of the information needed for the event. Print cover on glossy photo paper and the inside on thick matte photo paper.

DIRECTIONS

1. In your page layout software, create a series of text boxes that each measure 2 ⅛ " wide × 7 ⅝" tall (6 cm × 19.5 cm).

2. Scan the images from page 76, or find some suitable clip art images. Import them into the documents and center each one at the top of the corresponding text boxes.

3. Write the invitation, directions, and reception information. (We used ACaslon Regular Small Caps for the font.) For the cover, pivot the text so it runs along the long edge. Leave plenty of room at the bottom so the text does not run too close to the screw post. We wrote "weddings" in a sans serif font to mimic the style of the booklet that inspired this invitation. We also added the year "04" in the space where the trademark usually sits.

4. Print the cover on glossy photo paper. Print the inserts on a thick matte photo paper. Trim to size. Round the corners with a corner punch.

5. Punch a hole in the lower left corner, ¼" (.5 cm) from the edges. If your hole punch is too large for the screw post shaft, use a star-shaped punch and some of the interior corners will provide friction.

TIP *Make sure that the paper fills the length of the screw post shaft. If the paper you have chosen is too thin to fill up the length of the shaft, you can use an eyelet in place of the screw post. You can then thread a key ring through the eyelet and add a charm.*

MATERIALS

personal computer

scanner

color printer

page layout software (such as Quark or PageMaker)

images (see the templates on page 76)

scissors

ruler

hole punch

curvy corner punch

short nickel-plated screw posts

glossy photo paper

thick matte photo paper

Cork Popper

CHAMPAGNE BOTTLE LABEL

MATERIALS

personal computer

page layout
software
(such as Quark
or PageMaker)

color printer

colored paper

paper trimmer

PVA glue,
neutral adhesive,
or Fast Tack

Granted, if you are inviting hundreds of people to your wedding, the postage for this invite alone would be formidable. Let's be fair, this may not faze you at all, or it may leave you sitting with your head between your knees. However, for a smaller wedding, or one that is focused on a certain feeling (think tuxedos, New Year's Eve, and decadence), sometimes a little extra hits the mood just right. Buy half-bottles of your favorite champagne (see, we're showing a little restraint) and cover the labels with an invitation. Leave the real label intact underneath so people can know what they're drinking as they toast your impending nuptials (because that's the idea with this kind of an invitation). We mimicked the border treatment of the real label, and printed the invitation on a paper that matched the label.

DIRECTIONS

1. Measure the label on the bottle. Create a text box on your computer that measures ¼" (0.5 cm) larger in both dimensions. Set the invitation wording in the text box.

2. Print the invitation on the paper. Trim to size. We used vellum on our invitation and glued two layers together to achieve the proper opacity. If you are using a regular paper, you will probably not need to layer the paper.

3. Make sure the surface of the bottle is clean and free from grease. Run a thin bead of glue around the edges of the invitation and carefully center on the bottle label. Smooth the invitation onto the bottle and hold in place for a few second to let the glue set.

TIP *Check mailing laws for the states and countries you will be mailing to. Buy some sparking cider or other non-alcoholic beverage for those places that will not accept alcohol—or to send to those friends who don't drink the hard stuff.*

Longevity

ESSENTIAL FOR MARRIAGE BUT NOT FOR INVITATIONS

When you buy a black dress or sling-back shoes, you may consider how classic the design is. If that dress has a little Audrey Hepburn to it, you are pleased that the style will endure and that you will get years of use from its classic form. If you buy an expensive suit, you consider how wearable it will be five years down the line. That's a smart way to think—when you are dealing with items you will use repeatedly.

Your invitation is one-time-use only. Sure, you may keep it tucked away someplace safe and reminisce about the wedding day when you uncover it. Your friends, however, probably do not have such long-term plans for the invitation, no matter how much thought you put into it. Your best bet is to treat an invitation like a piece of performance art rather than a gallery piece. It will fulfill its duty and be done.

There's no need to be shackled to a classic design just because it will withstand the test of time. If you and your sweetheart want something a little witty, goofy, or out of the ordinary, don't fret about how it will look in twenty years. You are meant for the next twenty years, but your invitations are good only until the main event. And so what if someone keeps the invitation and occasionally rags you about how your style was so 2004? Quel compliment! Now that is impact.

Likewise, it's no reason to chuck convention out the window if that fits your style the best. You don't have to take advantage of an invitation's short tenure just because you can—only do so if it suits you.

The same style sense that tells you which clothes to buy will also inform your choice of invitation, but you are no doubt able to take that style to a more outlandish point, if that's your desire. There's no point in choosing a sedate invitation for fear of how it will look in twenty years. If you stick to your sense of self, style, and personality, you won't have any trouble.

If you *are* thinking down the long line, consider how fantastic your style is already, and how it is supposed to change over time. Don't believe us? Go to your closet. Way in the back. See those outfits you couldn't possibly give away, but couldn't bear to wear? They were perfect once, but they wouldn't do you any favors now. But you still love them for how perfectly they suited you then. Same goes for invitation and wedding decisions. We can't always please who we will be decades from now, but we will have a better chance of wonderful memories if we relax and live it up now. Longevity may be the goal of a marriage, but don't eschew the delights of the temporal when planning the invitation style and wedding details. People would much rather see your excitement and style bursting through an invitation that may not suit you in a few years than receive something that says nothing about you and your intended.

What to Say

GETTING THE WORDS RIGHT

Invitation wording gets a lot of attention. You will no doubt have noticed the many explanation of just what to write. So why are we tackling that, too, when so many others have? A wedding invitation is still an invitation, and not an immovable document where only the names change. Please! While it requires the inclusion of basic necessary information, it does not have to conform to a standard spelling or wording if you don't want it to.

Etiquette books make a good read. They are almost like novels in their fascinating twists and situations. They are reliable, but not infallible, and there is no reason to shun their advice out of some misguided inclination that etiquette is boorish. Proper etiquette is not snobbery. We turn to these books to learn how to put people at ease, make a graceful expression, and treat people with respect. That makes sense. We know some people who read them for sheer curiosity (okay, okay, guilty!). After all, you might run into the Dalai Lama or a Supreme Court justice, and you'll enjoy the encounter all the more if you know how to greet them in a way that is familiar and comfortable for them. (For that matter, you want to know how to make proper introductions or seat people at a party for maximum enjoyment.) However, following style books to the letter disallows your own graceful creativity. Keep in mind that they are called "guides," not "rule books." They are meant to help you wade through waters you might be nervous about; they are not meant to make you an unwilling manners puppet.

There are several books that will provide you with elaborate explanations of wedding invitation wording. Not all of the guidance will agree. That's okay, because that's what personal style is for, baby! *Here are the basics:*

1. Include the who, what, where, when, and any "how" that might be necessary, such as "ice skating to follow" or "summer hats welcome."

2. Traditional wording and spelling includes requesting the "honour" of someone's presence with the time and date spelled out completely.

3. An invitation is issued by the hosts. That's why many invitations start off with the names of the bride's parents: "Mr. and Mrs. Philippe Hughes are thrilled to invite you to the marriage of their daughter . . . ." More and more couples are hosting their own weddings, however, so the wording can come directly from the couple: "Our joy will be more complete if you join with us, Marjorie Allen and Trevor LaTourelle, in our marriage on . . . ."

4. The year is not necessary in an invitation, because the date is in the near future.

We got hitched!
Tim & Kim Gray

3.15.2003

A Thousand Words

GIGANTIC PHOTO SLIDE

Let people in on a moment from your honeymoon with a giant photo slide. Instead of showing people an entire slideshow of your trip, this card pokes a little fun at that (dare we say boring?) tradition. This card works as a thank-you note and shares with recipients a little about where you went and some of what you did. It also works brilliantly as an announcement that you eloped. Subtly funny, the slide offers a retro-style way to share your memories with people you love.

DIRECTIONS FOR SLIDE

1. Create a new document in your page layout program 4 ¾" (11.5 cm) square.

2. Create a 3 ½" wide × 3" deep (9 cm × 8 cm) picture box and import the photograph into your document from your compact disc. Leave about 1" (3 cm) on the bottom for your type and center the picture box left and right in your document.

3. Size picture to fit box.

4. Add your personalized text to the bottom of the page as shown in the photo.

5. Print the document onto transparency film at 104 percent.

6. Trim newly created transparency slide with craft knife, leaving about ¼" (0.5 cm) around outside edge of image area.

7. Load printer with a sheet of card stock and output two copies of the document, this time at 100 percent.

8. Cut both copies out and die-cut the corners with the rounded corner punch.

VARIATION *Insert one of these slides into an envelope with a thank-you card. Make the thank-you card the same proportions and use the corner punch to mirror the giant slide.*

MATERIALS

photo from your honeymoon on a compact disc

8 ½" × 11" (22 cm × 28 cm) inkjet or laser transparency film (to match your printer)

8 ½" × 11" (22 cm × 28 cm) inkjet or laser card stock

personal computer

page layout software (such as Quark or PageMaker)

color printer

craft knife

metal ruler

pencil

rounded corner punch

glue stick

snazzybags.com silver envelope 5" × 7 ¼" (13 cm × 20 cm)

fig. 1

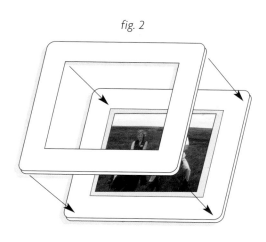

9. Cut out center windows on both copies. You have just created the frame for the slide.

10. Center, then adhere transparency to back of frame with glue stick *(see fig. 1)*.

11. Center, then adhere back of frame to front of frame with glue stick *(see fig. 2)*.

DIRECTIONS FOR SLIDE EASEL

1. Photocopy the easel template from page 77 and cut out the photocopy.

2. Place a piece of the card stock on your work surface. Place template over card stock and trace around outside edges. Cut out newly created card-stock easel.

3. Fold, then glue tab to back of card *(see fig. 3)*.

4. Place in silver envelope.

5. Create mailing labels for the outside envelope using a mailing label system, such as Avery, or handwrite them yourself onto an adhesive-backed label.

fig. 3

fig. 2

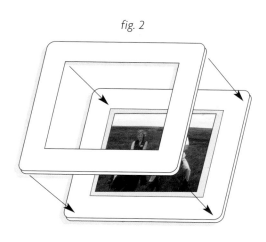

We got hitched!
Tim & Kim Gray
3.15.2003

Refrigerator Reminder

MAGNETIC SAVE-THE-DATE CARD

What good is a save-the-date card if you can never find it? Losing things (pieces of paper, say) doesn't necessarily make you disorganized. There is just so much to keep track of sometimes that even the happiest bits of mail get buried. It happens to the best of us, including your nearest and dearest. Give your guests half a chance. This card is magnetic and will make a stylish and functional addition to the fridge door. Along with the message, the wedding date is circled on a small calendar, making it an extra-effective reminder.

DIRECTIONS

1. Create an 8 ½" × 11" document in your page layout program.

2. Draw a rectangle 4" wide × 6" deep (10 cm × 15 cm) on the page.

3. Scan icon, save as a .tiff file, and place on page.

4. Color icon maroon.

5. Create stripes of varying thickness in background and color them lime green, orange, and pink.

6. Set type for reminder.

7. Duplicate the card and place it next to the other one, so you can print two up at a time (see fig. 1).

8. Print onto card stock or glossy photo paper.

9. Trim and place in plexiglass frame.

10. Wrap in pink tissue and place in envelope.

VARIATION *Thanks to adhesive magnet sheets, you can make a true magnet out of your paper card. Simply print the card, peel back the magnetic sheet's protective paper, and press the card onto the magnet sheet, smoothing any air bubbles away with a bone folder.*

MATERIALS

4" wide × 6" deep (10 cm × 15 cm) plexiglass frame with magnet on back

personal computer

scanner

color printer

page layout software (such as Quark or PageMaker)

8 ½" × 11" (22 cm × 28 cm) laser or inkjet card stock or glossy photo paper

4 ¼" × 6 ½" (10.5 cm × 17 cm) lime green vellum envelope

clip art of wedding location or representative icon

pink tissue paper

Tea and Camaraderie

TEA PARTY INVITATION

MATERIALS

personal computer

scanner

color printer

page layout software
(such as Quark
or PageMaker)

templates from
page 76

8 ½" × 11"
(22 cm × 28 cm)
cream-colored laser
or inkjet card stock

craft knife

metal ruler

bone folder

glue stick

tea bag

stapler

scissors

5 ¾" (14.5 cm)
square light
blue envelope

Showers come in many forms, from strobe-light-accompanied nights on the town to comparatively sedate get-togethers where friends can chat or catch up on the latest. A tea party is a perfect example of the latter. Tea, sandwiches, cookies, and—best of all—a chance to hang out with your pals. This invitation sums it up with a hands-on icon. The style is reminiscent of dreamy Italian moderne posters and gives the clear hint that the tea party won't be a trip into a world of ultraproper, pinky-raising tea sipping. And don't forget, more and more showers are for the couple, instead of just the bride. This invitation has enough of a masculine edge to suit a couple's shower as well.

DIRECTIONS

1. Create an 11" wide × 8 ½" deep (28 cm × 22 cm) document in your page layout program.

2. Scan in template from page 76 at 200 percent and save as an eps file. Place eps in your document.

3. On back panel of the placed template, typeset the words for the invitation.

4. Print out invitation from your color printer onto the cream-colored card stock.

5. Using your craft knife and metal ruler, cut out the invitation.

6. Cut slit in teacup following black line provided in template.

7. Lightly score fold areas lightly with craft knife and ruler *(see fig. 1 on page 66).*

TIP *Use a nice tea bag for this invitation. Go to the store and buy a couple of tea varieties (you can drink them, after all) in your quest to find a nice-looking tea bag with a nice tag. You may already drink a variety that fits the design perfectly (we like Twinings), but if not, do a little research for optimal impact.*

You're Invited

8. Fold in flap edges *(see fig. 2)* and burnish with the bone folder.

9. Glue flap edges with glue stick and adhere front to back panels *(see fig. 3)*.

10. Scan "you're invited" tea tag from page 76 in at 100 percent, then print and cut out.

11. Cut off the existing tag from a tea bag and staple "you're invited" tag to the tea bag string, tying off a knot around the staple, leaving 3" (8 cm) of string hanging from tea bag to tea tag.

12. Trim end of string with scissors and place tea bag into card.

13. Fill out card and place into blue envelope.

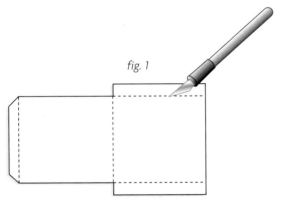

fig. 1

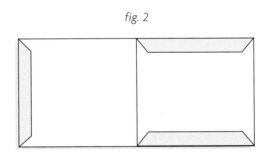

fig. 2

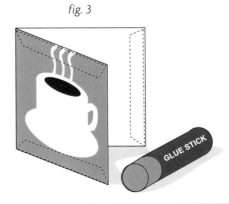

fig. 3

Please join us for a

Bridal Shower & Tea

honoring
Lynne Waring

Sunday, January 18, 2004
at eleven a.m.

100 Lake Point
Swansea, Mass.

PLEASE R.S.V.P. TO KARINA BY JANUARY 5
(401) 299-3434

Lynne's
Peppermint
Herbal Tea

VARIATION *For a different look, you can make your own tea wrapper, with requisite invitation information placed directly on the packaging.*

Where in the World?

DESTINATION INVITATION

MATERIALS

4 ½" × 6"
(11 cm × 15 cm)
tag with grommet

small red hang tag
with grommet

copyright-free country
map of wedding location

10" (25 cm) length of
off-white cord

personal computer

scanner

color printer

templates from page 77

8 ½" × 11" (22 cm × 28 cm)
white labels for your
type of printer

page layout program
(such as Quark or
PageMaker)

coordinating envelopes
for big tag and little tag

deckled-edge scissors
or rotary paper
trimmer with deckled-
edge rotary blade

scissors

craft knife

triangle

spray mount adhesive

Destination weddings are increasingly popular. And for good reason—they're a blast. Everyone is from out of town and ready for adventure. And what an adventure a wedding is to begin with. Why not go the extra step and involve Rio, Hawaii, or Tuscany? Point guests to the destination with these travel-themed "luggage tags." The mounting excitement of a trip to take part in a friend's wedding is enhanced by the brightly colored tags and retro luxury liner logos.

DIRECTIONS FOR FRONT OF INVITATION

1. Create a 4 ½" wide × 4" deep (11 cm × 10 cm) document in your page layout program.

2. Scan or find website of appropriate map and place it into your page layout program. Set the type "You are here" in white and place over an arrow dingbat (in this case, we used a Zapf Dingbat.) Color the arrow red so it is very visible.

3. Print out the map onto an 8 ½" × 11" (22 cm × 28 cm) sheet of label paper and trim it to size with deckled-edge scissors or rotary paper trimmer (outfitted with the deckled-edged blade).

4. Place 4 ½" × 6" (11 cm × 15 cm) tag on work surface, grommet facing left. Center map label on rectangular area of tag and adhere.

DIRECTIONS FOR BACK OF INVITATION

1. Color photocopy or scan the larger ticket template from page 77 and place onto 8 ½" × 11" (22 cm × 28 cm) adhesive label paper.

2. Trim to size with craft knife and ruler (or rotary trimmer with straight edge blade) and place on back of 4 ½" × 6" (11 cm × 15 cm) tag.

3. Loop cording through tag hole, knot, and trim ends.

4. Handwrite card with appropriate information and place in large envelope.

you are here

DIRECTIONS FOR RSVP

1. Color photocopy or scan the smaller ticket template from page 77 and place onto an 8 ½" × 11" (22 cm × 28 cm) adhesive label paper.

2. Trim to size.

3. Adhere to smaller red hang tag.

4. Loop cording through tag hole, knot, and trim ends.

5. Place in smaller envelope.

TIP *You can substitute a street map of the wedding location instead of the country map.*

flip your calendar
and save-the-date

PROJECT DESIGN: CHRISTINE TRAULICH, WWW.REDBLISS.COM

Flip-Flop Plan

BEACH-Y SAVE-THE-DATE CARD

Few things say summer and beach time like a bright pair of flip-flops. The breezy—and delightfully kitchy—attitude that this save-the-date card conveys reflects the casual and vibrant atmosphere you will no doubt achieve at your wedding festivities. Think drinks with little umbrellas, think fire-dancing luau performers, think clam bake rehearsal dinner, think the ultimate in beach fun. With a card that is elegant in its humorous references, guests will be prepared to be a little windswept and sandblown as they attend the joining of equal, carefree minds in a ceremony by the sea. Flip-flops are the footwear of the playful and at-ease types, so opt for a different icon if you are looking for ultimate seaside refinement.

DIRECTIONS

1. Cut Neutron blue cardstock into 5 ½" (14 cm) squares.

2. Cut yellow Razzle cardstock into 4 ½" (11 cm) squares.

3. Cut white Cryogen fold over cards down to 4 ½" (11 cm) squares.

4. Create a document 4 ½" wide × 8 ½" deep (11 cm × 22 cm) in your favorite page layout program. Set text for the front and inside of the save-the-date card and colorize text blue.

5. Print front and inside of card onto the white Cryogen fold-over cards.

6. Assemble and spray adhere the layers in the following order: Neutron blue (bottom), yellow Razzle (middle), white Cryogren (top).

7. Adhere flip-flops to the top of the fold-over card.

8. Place card in envelope.

VARIATION *Choose an icon from nature to convey a quieter, coastal to-do. Use a small starfish, sand dollar, or scallop shell, and guests will anticipate a more sedate, pristine, and refined occasion.*

MATERIALS

8 ½" × 11" (22 cm × 28 cm) blue Neutron card stock

8 ½" × 11" (22 cm × 28 cm) yellow Razzle card stock

A2 white Cryogen fold-over cards

5 ¾" (14.5 cm) blue envelopes

1" (3 cm) foam flip-flops

color printer

page layout program (such as Quark or PageMaker)

paper cutter or craft knife and ruler

spray adhesive

We Eloped!

POST-GETAWAY ANNOUNCEMENT

MATERIALS

8 ½" × 14"
(22 cm × 36 cm)
white laser or inkjet
card stock

postage stamp from
wedding destination

inking stamp from
wedding destination

inkpad with brown ink

jpeg honeymoon photo

personal computer

page layout software
(such as Quark
or PageMaker)

photo manipulation
software (such as
Photoshop)

scanner

color printer

5 ¼" (14.5 cm)
square pale
green envelope

photo corners

bone folder

craft knife

glue stick

Think that escaping for a matrimonial getaway leaves you craftless? Think again! Any invitation listed in this book can be adapted to create a stunning announcement of your nouveau marital status. This announcement, however, is specially designed for those of you who do not want to go through the full-on wedding planning. No matter how you usher in your marriage, share the joy and a glimpse into your sneak attack on wedded bliss.

DIRECTIONS

1. Scan postage stamp into your computer at about 200 percent. Save as an .eps file.

2. Import image into Photoshop or equivalent program.

3. Set the type in Photoshop and colorize.

4. Rotate the photo 7 degrees clockwise.

5. Create a new document in your page layout program 4" (10 cm) square.

6. Place the stamp .eps into the center of the document, and scale it up until it measures 2 ½" (6 cm) wide.

7. Trim document to size.

8. Create a separate document in your page layout program 4" deep × 12" wide (10 cm × 30 cm). Divide into three equal sections making the first section pale blue, the second one olive green, and the third one pale blue.

9. Place photo corners around a photo of you and your spouse and scan as a tiff file.

VARIATION *If you don't have a stamp from your destination, consider using a tacky postcard or souvenir. Forgot to get one? (We know, you were busy.) Check out eBay or your favorite "kitsch" shop if your destination is culturally popular, like Hawaii or the Caribbean.*

10. Import image into the the first blue panel of your document and scale until it is 3" (8 cm) wide. Center on page.

11. Type message in panel 2.

12. Print and then trim to size.

13. Stamp with inking stamp from destination on panel 3.

14. Fold and score at color breaks with bone folder so it makes a Z-fold with three separate sections.

15. Glue stick the front cover and burnish it to back side of the first panel of the Z-fold.

16. Stamp exterior envelope with destination ink stamp on front and back.

How Many Prizes Are Inside?

THE ELEMENTS OF AN INVITATION

Strictly speaking, any invitation should contain only an invitation, a reply card, and a stamped envelope for the reply card. All three elements should be contained in the main envelope. Directions and other information should be sent separately after the response is received.

Tradition has dictated that formal invitations be sent in a double envelope. That means that the outer envelope that is marked up and dirtied by its trip through the postal system is opened to reveal a pristine envelope that contains the invitation and reply materials. This double envelope harkens back to the days when footmen delivered messages by hand. The outer envelope was susceptible to flecks of mud from the dirt street, finger prints, footprints, you name it. The outer envelope was discarded at the recipient's house, revealing an impeccable envelope with only the intended person's name on it (after all, the footman had delivered it to the proper address, so the house number was no longer needed). That style of packaging has remained somehow. Although it's unlikely that a clod of dirt will be chucked up from a passing horse cart onto the invitation envelope, the pure and clean interior envelope is like a drum roll. You know you are about to open something important. It's exciting! Today, that inside envelope still has only the names of the recipients on it, with no address. Essentially, the postal service is acting as an automated and expert footman. It's a cleaner process all round these days, so don't feel wedded to the double enclosure if you think it's over the top.

That amounts to five pieces of paper: the outer envelope, the inner envelope, the invitation, the reply card, and the envelope for the reply card. And yet, most of the invitations we've received over the years have been packed tighter than a sausage with maps, directions, messages, cards to fill with memories, lists of

hotels, and so on. Including these pieces assures that you won't forget to send it later. But there is a trade-off to consider fully before making that choice. Packing the invitation with all the extras draws a lot of attention away from the invitation. The double envelope sets the stage for an impact, but the gorgeous invitation you made may easily be lost in a world of photocopied maps or hotel lists.

There are some things you can do to keep the focus on the invite:

- Prepare a second mailing with all of the extra information. Send it immediately after the invitation, or wait until you receive people's responses.
- Don't use photocopies. The full-size sheet is often folded into thick quarters and shoved into the envelope, taking up room and hiding the more beautiful elements. The ink from the photocopy flakes off along the folds.
- If you would like to include the extras with the invitation, scan any images or maps into the computer. Type messages to accompany them and keep the size down. Make the info documents twice the size of the invitation (at the most) and fold them cleanly in half so they fit easily into the envelope. Do not print anything on the fold line.

- Incorporate the invitation additions into the invitation design. Instead of making them seem like an add-on, make them belong.
- Use a large enough envelope. If you are putting a lot of items into an envelope, make it easy and smooth, not a demonstration in cramming and paper cuts. When in doubt, choose an envelope that's a bit larger and make it easier for your guests to slide out your invitation.

Invitation stuffing may not be ideal, but it may be the best choice for you. Consider how to make the information succinct and effective, as well as unobtrusive. Simple information always trumps a novella in this case. And if you're adding things in, don't forget that your add-ins can go beyond the usual information. You could add a card into the invitations of people with kids encouraging them to bring their lovely offspring—and a change of clothes for the afternoon of games. You could include an invitation to a brunch the next morning, as that might affect some people's early-made travel plans. Dream it up, but keep it to the point and small. And if you can resist, let the invitation do its job before showering people with all the minor details.

Swatch Us Get Hitched, page 52

Templates

✳

Great free art you can copy directly from this book

You're Invited

Tea and Camaraderie, page 64

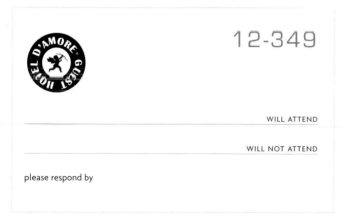

12-349

WHO:

WHAT:

WHEN:

WHERE:

reception to follow

12-349

WILL ATTEND

WILL NOT ATTEND

please respond by

Where in the World?, page 68

A Thousand Words, page 58

Curvy embrace, page 22

Resources

Where to find the goods to make these cool projects

*

About the Authors

Laura McFadden is a freelance art director living in Somerville, Massachusetts. She is a former design director for *Inc.* magazine. She currently runs her own graphic design studio, Laura McFadden Design, Inc., and has contributed to various craft books and magazines for publishers such as Rockport Publishers, Martingale & Company, and *Handcraft Illustrated*. She is a coauthor, with April Paffrath, of *The Artful Bride: Simple, Handmade Wedding Projects* (Rockport, 2003).

April Paffrath is a freelance editor and writer in Cambridge, Massachusetts. In addition to book and magazine editing, she has written architecture profiles, travel pieces, cooking articles, and craft how-to's for magazines such as *Scientific American Explorations* and *Martha Stewart Living*. She is a coauthor, with Laura McFadden, of *The Artful Bride: Simple, Handmade Wedding Projects* (Rockport, 2003).

Acknowledgments

Once again, we'd like to thank Silke Braun, Regina Grenier, MaryAnn Hall, Ann Fox, Winnie Prentiss, and all of the other great people at Rockport Publishers for their continued support.

Also, thanks very much to my friends Kristin Bradetich, Kim Gray, Kevin Miller, and Lynne G. Waring; my sister-in-law and cohort in crafts, Andrea Renzi McFadden; my neighbor and constant supporter, Anna Herrick; Christine Traulich of Red Bliss, and all of the people who contributed their great ideas and time. —LM

Dedication

To my two boys, Matthew and Ray, you are my reason to be. —LM

To my favorite person, my husband Matthew. Thanks for breakfast. —AP